INSCAPE

2021

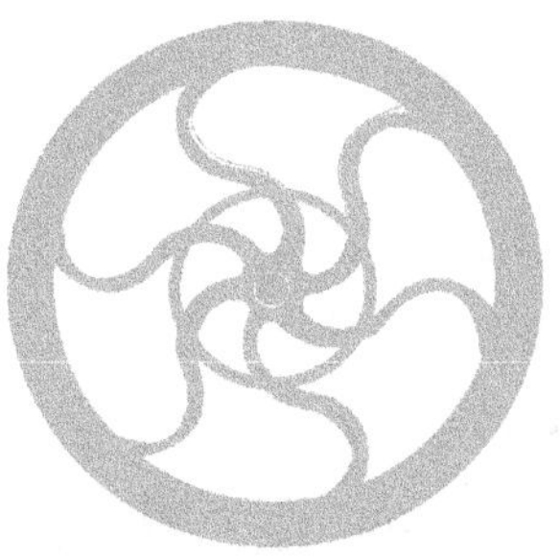

WASHBURN UNIVERSITY
Department of English
1700 SW College Ave
Topeka, KS 66621

Thank you Washburn University Department of English.

Vol. 46

inscapemagazine.org

washburn.edu/inscape

facebook.com/inscapemagazine

Cover Art: The Aperture by Sonnet Mondal

Inscape, compiled annually at Washburn University in Topeka, Kansas, features poetry, fiction, nonfiction, and visual art from the region and beyond.

INSCAPE
2021

CO-EDITORS

Mack Grimes & Shelby Hanson

MAGAZINE DESIGN

McKenzie McCoy-Smoot

FACULTY ADVISOR

Andrew Farkas

CONTENTS

EDITORS' CHOICE

FICTION

81 *Slow* MADISON JOZEFIAK

NONFICTION

11 *Genealogy* GABRIEL BLACKWELL

POETRY

13 *At Night in a Garden* K. BRANAGAN

6 *Body as a Second Language* JULIANA CHANG

8 *Non Sequitur* GABRIEL BLACKWELL

10 *Change* GABRIEL BLACKWELL

15 *Azore Man* ARTHUR DAVIS

25 *End Call* ELIZABETH MOORE

26 *BFRB* ELIZABETH MOORE

27 *Hansel & Gretel* BRADLEY R. STRAHAN

30 *Miranda Miranda* BROOKE WONDERS

34 *In Sickness, Health, and Space-Time* BRIANNA NOLL

36 *Partitoned Space* BRIANNA NOLL

37 *Surviving Linear Time* BRIANNA NOLL

38 *Missive on an Old Refutation of Time* JOACHIM GLAGE

41 *Tree Envy* LIERIN WOODS

42 *The Storm-King and the Tree Below* GREGOR SOUTHARD

44 *A Room Alone with Birds* K. BRANAGAN

45	*Ain't No Virgin on the Rocks*	K. BRANAGAN
46	*She Dances with Death*	K. BRANAGAN
47	*Guitar*	EVAN MCHENRY
48	*Untitled #4*	JEREMY SZUDER
49	*Untitled #7*	JEREMY SZUDER
50	*Untitled #18*	JEREMY SZUDER
51	*The Tomb and the Door*	SONNET MONDAL
52	*Book Signings*	GREGOR SOUTHARD
54	*Deb Sanders's Etch a Sketches*	MICHAEL MARTONE
55	*Jim O'Day's Folly*	MICHAEL MARTONE
56	*My Grandfather's Hog Oiler*	MICHAEL MARTONE
57	*Falling*	MICHAEL BUCKIUS
58	*Squab*	JAMES TADD ADCOX
59	*Van Gogh on Suicide Prevention*	HOLLIE DUGAS
60	*Food for Thought*	JAMES ROGERS
68	*The Sun and the Marsh Played Strategy Games*	RYAN BOLLENBACH
69	*The Sun as a Child*	RYAN BOLLENBACH
71	*A Giant Is Always Interrupting: Giant Bernard's Name Has Changed to Protect His Past*	BRIAN OLIU
72	*Falling Among Crows*	ANNA E. CHILDS
74	*Phantasmagoric Truth*	ANNA E. CHILDS
76	*Thickets*	ANNA E. CHILDS
78	*To Barbara Kruger: My Battlefield*	ANNA E. CHILDS
92	*The Terrorists*	MARISA P. CLARK
94	*Contributors*	

BODY AS A SECOND LANGUAGE

Juliana Chang

I.

I am not well versed in the ways my body
speaks as someone else. I know the skin
and eyes must come from somewhere.
I know my body did not invent its own fear.
I know fear looks like fists and flushed cheeks to me
for a reason. Some stories take two generations
to truly tell.

II.

Most of my hurt was born
before this body knew its name.
I've held it in my bones my whole life. And yet,
when the stories come out, years and years later,
I sprout six tongues of ink in my anger.
Neither of us were built to live like this,
even if we bury his face in all the right words.
Even if we spend the rest of time trying.

III.

Over the phone, she begs me
not to make the same mistakes she did.
I agree, tell her to call, anytime, whatever she needs.
I want to hurt him back. I want to ask her to come here,

come stay with me,
but the question turns to ash in my mouth.

IV.

Come stay with me. Everything else has already arrived.
I inherited the silence, but the fire as well.
I know my body did not invent its own strength.
I want to keep you safe. I love you.
I am always, always,
growing towards you.

NON SEQUITUR

Gabriel Blackwell

First thing that came to my mind when my girlfriend and I decided to have a gender reveal party, the man has said, *were alligators.* He was explaining why he had been seen—over five million times—placing a watermelon filled with blue Jell-O in an alligator's mouth. This was in a video, on Facebook. When the same video was shared on Twitter, almost immediately, concerns were raised. Was the alligator being mistreated? Exploited? Clearly, it was being exploited, but was it also being mistreated? What about those two children in the background? It couldn't possibly be safe for them to be there. The man, though, the father, by now, of a son, one supposes, says he *prepared for numerous scenarios in which things could have gone wrong.* And anyway, this was not simply an alligator, it was a part of the family. The man's grandfather had raised the alligator, a female named Sally, from an egg. There had been no explosion at this party like the one that produced the shrapnel that killed the grandmother-to-be in Iowa. Nothing that happened sparked a massive wildfire, as at parties in Arizona and California. Instead, the alligator closed its mouth around the watermelon and a blue substance nearly the same hue as the man's immense shirt shot out onto the ground next to the man's olive Crocs. Above the two, in the frame, are ten or eleven men and women, all pointing their phones at the alligator, Sally. The only one without a phone is the mother-to-be. Actually? She seems nervous. A decade before, a different pregnant woman, wanting to bake and eat a cake but without an occasion that would call for one, invented the gender reveal party. Of course this doesn't explain why the idea proved so popular. But now, this same woman is on the record as being against gender reveal parties. It had been a silly thing she did and then posted on social media, she says. It shouldn't become some ritual, she says. She doesn't like that it reinforces the prevailing binary, this or that, blue or pink, she says. Because I am distracted—my mother-in-law is here, having fled the fires in her home state—I spent nearly an entire day this week turning over, in the back of my mind, the question of what to call this tendency I see everywhere online of people arguing with others who have claimed that a thing has some particular quality that, no, that thing has this other quality instead, always as though the thing in question cannot have both the one particular quality and the other quality, too. This is a logical fallacy, I know, an obvious logical fallacy, but which fallacy is it? Lately, I have trouble with basic facts like this one—I know a thing has a name or suspect that a thing has a name, but I'm unable to come up with the name I'm sure it has. This is made more frustrating, in this case, because people have decided to call this tendency *whataboutism,* an awkward and even ugly name, meant, one guesses, to be mocking, but, freed of its specific context, it only makes those saying it seem slow-witted. (Maybe, though, I think, changes in language always seem slow-witted at their conception. Did Shakespeare's audiences laugh at his coinages, all those un-s, and think, *Well, what do you expect from the son of a glover*? Is *glover,* I wonder, only a corruption of glove-maker or is it also more elegant?) It isn't even that this tendency expresses a want or a need for everything to be either one thing or another, but that it expresses a want or a need for everything to be perfectly distillable down to metonymy. One almost wants to call this the seed of every conspiracy, this tendency, a lazy way of thinking about complex things. In writing, isn't the saying, *First thought, best thought*?

CHANGE

Gabriel Blackwell

There is a letter from Milena Jesenska to Max Brod on the subject of Franz Kafka that has stayed with me even long after I first read it. In this letter, Milena writes that Kafka is like a man who, having written a telegram, goes to the telegram office, approaches the window only after thinking carefully about which window he ought to use, turns over his telegram and the money required to send it, and then, upon receiving his change, walks slowly away, counting the change. When he discovers he has been given too much change, he goes back to the window to return the portion not due him. And then, on the street, having left the office, he looks again at the change he was given, discovers that, no, in fact he was given the correct change and has thus given back a portion of the change due him, and then returns to the telegram office, claiming that, while the mistake was his, it is the principle of the thing he is now pursuing in demanding what he'd returned be returned to him. But a strange thing happens in this letter—Milena begins the story by saying something along the lines of what I've said here, that Kafka is a man *like* such a man, but after she has finished telling this story she makes an allusion to *the incident*, indicating that it really happened. I suppose the whole thing has stayed with me because of this switch at the end, from conditional—*if* this were to happen to "Frank" (she always calls Franz Kafka "Frank"), *then* he would act in this way—to historical: This happened to Frank.

GENEALOGY

Gabriel Blackwell

There is a section of nearly all biographies, at the beginning or near the beginning, where the author of the biography describes at the very least the lives of the biography's subject's mother and father, perhaps also the subject's siblings, if there are any, possibly also the subject's grandparents, even, in the most offensive examples, the subject's great-grandparents and perhaps even their great-great-grandparents. One struggles to come up with a precise analogue for this phenomenon—is it as though, in order to give the answer to a mathematical problem, one recited not only the problem, but also the principles behind the operation one performed to solve the problem as well as giving a brief summary of one's education in mathematics—but the end result is that the reader spends a good bit of time wanting to know about *the subject of the biography* and learning nothing about them. It is doubly frustrating that, most often, this comes *at the very beginning of the biography,* so that one sets out to learn something about someone, consults a biography, and learns nothing about that someone until first they have sat through a sometimes-complex genealogy. It can't be that the writers of biographies have never themselves read biographies, can it? Is it possible they've never themselves felt the urge to throw a book across the room for wasting their time so needlessly? It stands to reason that, if one wants to read a biography of the biography's subject's father, one ought to read a biography of the subject's father (and not a biography of the subject), and if one wants to write a biography of the subject's father, one ought to write a biography of the subject's father (and not a biography of the subject). One almost wants to only ever read biographies of orphans, merely to avoid having to read through interminable pages of data about people one cannot be made to care at all about. The trouble lies in the presumption that a history of a subject's family has anything to do with the life of the subject after they have left home. Undoubtedly, there are subjects whose families have had an outsized impact on them. But, even when it comes to such gargantuan figures as Kafka's father or Proust's mother, what really is the reader expected to learn from reading about the histories of these figures? Better to write about Kafka, about Proust, and, when necessary, about their lives with their fathers, mothers, siblings. Yesterday, I noticed our daughter, in her stroller, banging the back of her head against the hard plastic shell and told her to stop. She looked perfectly happy to be banging her head against the hard plastic shell, of course, but I knew that, eventually, the pain of what she was doing would catch up to her and she would begin crying, and then—and here we were, on the street, with downtown shoppers all around us—I would have to somehow console her for the consequences of her own actions, and the dull ache in the back of her head, I thought, would last all day, until her mother got home from work, and eventually, perhaps in a year, perhaps even further away in the future, they would both resent what they saw as my failures.

AT NIGHT IN A GARDEN

K. Branagan

A Hungarian witch watcher was walking
Through my dreams last night
He fired a slingshot message
Written in Hieroglyphics on watercolor
Paper in cigarette ash
Wrapped in a ripped off collar
Around a cherry pit
Tied together with dried tiger lily leaves.
It said *To Grow Sky Flowers* and had
A list of ingredients for seedling potting soil:

Peat moss
crushed scarab bones
petals from a secret planted cosmos
wood shavings from a red barn door
translucent stones from a tombstone garden
sugar water collected in the morning
in the palm of your hands

And there was a bastard garden growing in my backyard
So, I stopped tending it and I left

It for the earth to take
In exchange for the nocturnal
Treasure hunter's dreams of being,
Able to catch a fish out of water with nothing
On the calendar for the rest of my life
A golden apple map for a bookmark
Pressed like a dead flower petal
Between two coffins

AZORE MAN

Arthur Davis

I recognized him immediately, and yet not at all.

The startling odor emanating from his body was a mixture of decay and what could only be described as reptilian life.

"My name is Michael Warren," I had said, resting on a small log at the entrance to Miguel's hut and as far away as I could be from the man whose legs overhung the small wooden bed by almost a meter.

My editor had been correct, and I knew then that I would forever be indebted to his instincts, and to his trust in mine.

I had arrived a week ahead of my film crew to make final edits to our shooting schedule and get a more intimate sense of the sweep and nature of the Azores, an archipelago composed of nine volcanic islands in the Mid-Atlantic about 1,360 km west of Portugal.

I had just spent a year with another crew in the Democratic Republic of the Congo filming silverback mountain gorillas in brutal conditions that challenged the most veteran of the team, one whose right foot had to be amputated before filming was completed. This was going to be a vacation from that hell.

My plan to get organized and set up camp was interrupted by an urgent message from my editor to contact a local fisherman. He sensed there was more to the story than Miguel's exaggerated size of the man who had washed up near his hut yesterday.

As we hurriedly made our way up the beach, Miguel's translation of the incident and the size and condition of the man was soft spoken, but told with absolute certainty. After a few kilometers' hike, Miguel and I found two men, who he quickly described as distant cousins, blocking the entrance to his hut.

We approached slowly. "What are you doing here?" Miguel said to the taller man in his late forties sporting two gold teeth.

"We are family. We have every right as you do."

"You are criminals. You have been judged so by both sides of the family and our village."

"You can't keep us away. We saw what's inside and we have every right to be part of the reward for his return."

"I represent the British government," I said, removing my Government Authorization Permit from my pocket, validated by their state's official stamp. "I and I alone will decide who is to be credited and who will be judged to have interfered with Government business."

"We deserve to get part of the reward."

"If you continue to block the entrance to this hut, I will recommend to my government, as well as to yours, that you willfully interfered in my investigation. Now stand aside or I will call the authorities and have you both arrested."

They spoke to each other, then angrily to Miguel, who didn't flinch at what I could only make out were hardened threats. They finally left, but not before the taller one spat at the ground in front of where Miguel was standing.

"They are the worst of the evil that inhabits every village everywhere. We must be quick, as they will gather others," Miguel said, then cautiously pulled aside the flimsy curtain separating my world from his secret within.

The man's eyes were a radiant blue. He was covered in damp blankets foot to neck. Pails of seawater stood waiting at his bedside. "You are not with the other two men?"

"No," Miguel answered. "They left, but will be back."

"I understand some of your language. Thank you for what you did. What both of you did."

He looked me over and my name on the Wildlife Filming Permit the two thugs never got close enough to read. "Michael Warren, from wherever you came, I'm glad you're here. I don't know how much longer I could have held out." His English was precise and fitful. "My name is Daniel Gladstone. Sir Daniel Walter

Byron Gladstone."

Having nothing to go on but a frantic editor who had somehow been contacted by Miguel's brother was all I knew. "The world, including myself, thought you were dead?"

"You, and they, were more right than wrong."

The last transmission from his small, single-engine plane had come from 355 km south, southwest of the Azores. "You vanished two months ago. There was no trace of the wreckage. Nothing. Where have you been?"

"Out there," he said, barely able to nod in the direction of the sea beyond the confines of the hut.

His fingers were the longest I'd ever seen. There was a fringe of nascent webbing at the base between each digit connecting them in a pattern of translucent yellow-green.

"My back was badly injured in the crash. From the pain I guessed several vertebrae were crushed. Terrible headwinds and engine failure. I came ashore once on a fragment of a barren atoll, but standing and moving about was excruciating."

"So you went back into the ocean?"

"So I went back into the ocean, my only comfort a twisted branch of driftwood to cling to."

"I can't imagine."

"There were other wounds that caused me great pain, but the more I swam, the quicker they healed. I have little memory beyond what I've told you. I moved around an archipelago of small, unpopulated islands, but was never really far from shore. At first, such as it was, I found food in the tidal pools."

Sir Daniel Walter Byron Gladstone. The most able and unpolitical of his brethren, whose family could trace its ancestry and great fortune back to the charter that was granted by the British crown to the Hudson's Bay Company in the developing American colonies, had done the impossible.

Miguel's two unsavory cousins were going to do whatever it took to cash in on this discovery. Courtesies aside, we had no time to waste.

I offered him fresh water from my canteen, which he consumed through a series of painful and threatening gags as though he were poisoning himself.

“And?” was all I could muster.

“I swam around the boundaries of these volcanic islands, and the more I swam, the easier it was to swim, to remain for longer periods underwater, and for my body to tolerate such an unnatural environment. I ate whatever fish I caught. And the faster I swam, the more I caught.”

“The Azores?”

“I am Sir Daniel Gladstone of Beacham Manor, and all the land and titles appertaining there to,” he said as if we had just met, lifting himself up on one elbow, slowly letting his legs drop to the muddy floor as the rest of his body was unmasked by the blankets that fell into a pile.

Outside the hut, but within earshot, I could hear Miguel praying.

Gladstone was close to eight feet, and much of his skin was riddled with uncommon markings and deformities. His thighs were massive, belonging to a species that, as a nature photographer for close to three decades, had no equal.

What my editors hastily described as a “dying Englishman” without further detail or connection to the mysterious disappearance of Sir Daniel Gladstone, one of the leading scholars and philanthropists of the twenty-first century, left me in a state of relief, and disbelief.

“Please, there are doctors on the other islands that can help you.”

“Michael, is it?”

“Yes. Michael Warren. I’m here on assignment from the British Nature Preserve. The rest of my team will be here any day, and then we shoot for the next thirty days before we go back to London.”

“Except for Miguel there, who has sacrificed his own safety to protect and comfort me, I suspect those two villagers you first met have already spread rumors of my survival.”

“That’s what brought me here.”

“I am glad you were the first. You don’t seem like a man who would betray his countryman.”

“I would never...”

"...but there will be others who will insist on notifying the authorities and want to take me back."

"As well they should, as I should. You need medical treatment. You are barely alive."

"As a man, you would be correct. But only so."

Urgent voices outside the hut drew Miguel away.

"What are you saying?"

"On the second day after the crash I was stung by something. My body, already weakened and wracked with pain, became more inflamed. I could feel heat surge from my center as it exploded from the bite I sustained," he said, fumbling to pull away the remaining blankets.

Just below his sternum was a wound the size of a fist where he indicated he was stung, around which scar tissue was forming. There was a halo of red inflammation, but overall, it looked like it was healing. I imagined his constitution and the saltwater had something to do with this.

"And?"

"Besides this, I've been attacked by almost every fish and reptile looking for a quick meal. I fought them off with this," he said, producing a hunting knife from under the covers with a blade that had to be over twenty centimeters long.

"If I have the story straight, your father, William Jamison Gladstone, gave it to you on your fifteenth birthday."

"It saved my life many times over, but from the hundreds of bites my body absorbed toxic chemicals, powerful and transformative foreign proteins, so many that the changes I am undergoing are entirely unnatural. I graduated from Cambridge several decades ago at fourteen stone. Do you think I am fourteen stone now?"

"You look like a giant."

"A giant what?"

"I don't understand."

"Miguel found me on the beach. He moved his family out of here so he could tend to me. As I lay here, I can feel my human self dying. I need to get back into the ocean. It's the only place I have a chance to survive."

"If you're barely able to move here, you will certainly drown out there."

"Please, I need you to understand that whether or not I survive, what is happening cannot be reversed," he said, throwing back the last blanket.

I am a biologist by trade, a photographer by profession, and have been traveling the world almost since I could recall. I have no roots, nor do I feel the need to become a part of a family or community.

I have been part of several discoveries of unique species and many documented variations of animals we once took for granted. So surprise and grasping the nuances of natural transition is not uncommon. However, what I was witnessing could no longer be described by the vocabulary of modern science.

His legs had grown measurably and disproportionally longer than his upper torso, as if they belonged to another species entirely.

At first, I thought the small irregular squares that covered much of his lower body were moving. They weren't. They were growing, transforming, being reborn as nascent scales, a feature that out of its natural element would most certainly lead to death.

"If you think I have a choice, you would be wrong."

"You have a wife and three children. Aren't they a choice?"

He paused and considered my question. "At first, they were all that kept me alive. My beautiful wife and three blessed daughters. I don't remember much of them now and accept my fate for what it has become. To prolong that life would only bring terrible suffering to my family."

"And the pilot?"

"He was unconscious from the impact. I tried to revive him. If I'd held on to him longer, I would have drowned."

"I can't imagine."

"At first there was only survival and knowing that I couldn't withstand the terrible pain on land. I stayed close to the coast, and it was only in the last few days that I recall being thrown onto the rocky beach and this small village."

"Miguel said you were unconscious when he found you?"

"I swam in shock at first from the crash, finding it was easier to move my legs together, my body more undulating through the water than swimming. I can't describe it any other way. After a few weeks, together they propelled me through the water at an astonishing speed."

"And you're asking me to take you back into the ocean?"

"Michael, if you don't mind, I have crossed a point where I am more fish, or mid-species, than man, and ashore I will die as a curiosity to the world. In the water the transmutation might complete itself."

"Sir Gladstone?"

"William, please. Miguel saved my life and I'm asking you to do the same. I am dying. You can see it."

"I can," I finally admitted.

"Maybe this would help you understand," he said, pointing to a small growing ridgeline of wet, open flesh that started above his inner ankles and had already worked itself upwards toward his groin.

"What is it?"

"Biologically, I believe the ridgelines of each leg will draw the natural position of my legs together until..."

"Your legs fuse as one."

"They already undulate in the water together as if they were one."

"And the three rows of faint, pink slits under each side of your jaw?"

"You're very observant."

"Sir, I have dedicated my life to broaden and try to memorialize our understanding of species and try not to interfere within their natural habitat."

"Michael, please, there is no time left for logic. You have to suspend, as I already have, such traditional natural theories," he said and then heaved himself up from the bed and stiffened his weakened form so he was fully erect.

"Sir?"

"I beg of you, don't let me die here or let them take me away to spend the rest of my life as a living freak."

"I couldn't live with myself if by taking you back to the ocean I was somehow responsible for your death."

"Could you live with yourself if I wind up a lab curiosity and eternal embarrassment to my family and heritage?"

Miguel poked his head through the curtain and signaled me to come out, then he too noticed the giant standing in the middle of his hut. I could only speculate what that wound and the alien poisons his body had absorbed would result in when he was completely evolved.

"Go ahead," Gladstone gestured. "But we're running out of time."

"I thought he was going to die before you got here," Miguel explained in his broken English.

"He may die anyway."

"No, that's what I've come to tell you. Here there is help! A rescue! A rescue!" Miguel said, then tried to imitate the spiral movements of a helicopter.

"A helicopter?"

"Yes, yes," he said with great relief.

"Miguel, he needs our help to get him back into the ocean, now—this minute or he will die. You must believe me on this."

Gladstone, or what was left of him, shuffled out for the first time beyond the meager protection of Miguel's hut. He turned and looked back into the glare of the sun. I followed his gaze toward the black dot cruising closer.

"Hurry, wrap the wet blankets around me. The moisture will give me strength and conceal the truth of my transformation."

Miguel hesitated, then darted back into his hut and soaked a few blankets and wrapped the creature, whose balance was compromised as he moved toward the rocky coastline not fifty meters away.

A cluster of villagers inched toward us, and even before the helicopter could get close, I realized there was no place for it to land. That heartened and reenergized me while Miguel set his small frame against Sir Gladstone's massive hulk and, without pause, the three of us managed to reach the narrow stretch of beach that separated the rocky outcropping from the ocean.

Then, Miguel saw them first, screaming in the background. The two of them were racing towards us. This time the taller one with two gold teeth was waving a pistol overhead.

Gladstone pulled away from us and uttered something in a voice I will never forget, nor understand. It was high-pitched and guttural. He looked up into the heavens, rested a hand on my shoulder and one on Miguel's, again said something indistinguishable, then took a series of short, clumsy duck-steps and lunged forward into the waves.

Before he turned away for the last time, I could no longer recognize him as both eyes were now black as coal, darting frantically in every direction as he made his way home.

A fact that I'll take to my grave.

In the background, far away from where the villagers had collected, there were new, recognizable voices shouting commands and threats.

Miguel's life as well as mine were about to change forever, mostly for the worse as mankind collectively pitched itself behind what they would come to believe were traitors to both humanity and science.

"A miracle," Miguel said. "God's hand has blessed that man, and I believe we will see the likes of him again."

Sir William Gladstone's solicitor, a ferociously aggressive man flanked by two others who looked like they had once been Royal Marines, scrambled out of that first helicopter. Many others, less sympathetic and voraciously curious, were hours away.

The family's solicitor was rife with threats and warnings as to what he was prepared to do, as I had abetted the suicide of one of our nation's most revered figures.

After I escorted him into Miguel's hut and carefully explained what I had come upon and what had happened and the reasons for the urgent lifesaving decision I made, he questioned Miguel and saw the sincerity in the poor peasant's terrified eyes and the humanity behind our risk.

Shortly after the British authorities tried to arrest me, and most of the media pilloried me as a traitor, I was dismissed from my job. I made every detail of my experience clear to the public in one interview on the BBC, so that it would not be reinterpreted and distorted for unending theater and exploitation.

The world rose up to end me, though if they had seen the suffering and anguish and certainty in Sir Daniel Walter Byron Gladstone's stark, once lightning blue eyes, they would never have questioned my decision.

The Gladstones' solicitor reappeared, a changed man, months after the BBC interview.

In the kindest and most reassuringly grateful tone, he made it clear that Sir Daniel Gladstone's wife and family thanked me for my courage and for making an impossibly compassionate decision that had put my life and livelihood at risk; they would now put their great wealth and resources to my advantage.

A generous stipend had been arranged from which I and Miguel's family would receive a monthly sum. When I heard the breadth of their kindness, I knew I would never have to work another day in my life, and Miguel's family would be protected from all eventualities.

Before that second meeting concluded, the solicitor wanted me to know that the Gladstone family, and especially Sir Gladstone's wife's prayers, would forever be with me and thanked me for saving one of their most beloved. Embedded in that communiqué was a veiled request not to discuss or further publish any more details to the press or to the scientific community.

I've always considered my life a gift, doing what I liked, and somehow making a contribution to mankind's understanding of nature's infinite complexities and possibilities.

Eventually, I returned to the largest island in the Azores and have lived there these past twenty-three years.

But it was only when I met a brave fisherman who led me to the crystal blue stare of Sir Daniel Walter Byron Gladstone that I understood why I was put on this good earth.

END CALL

Elizabeth Moore

I think I loved her. In the space between my lungs and diaphragm.

The blue screen shined in the dark. The static made me think I could fall into it, into her. Hair twisted up by nervous fingers, her face blurry.

The weight of the laptop rested comfortably on my lap, the battery hot against my thigh. Wished it was the weight of her, the warmth of her.

Headphones in ears replay the sobs I pretended I couldn't hear. There were texts I pretended I couldn't read. Fingers were numb, stuck on keys, begging.

These days the whir of the computer sounds like her voice. The tags and posts remain frozen, a binary shrine to what used to be.

I don't check those accounts for fear there's a message and fear there isn't.

I remember her with an end call button hovering below, and I've been listening to a busy signal for three years now. Maybe I should have hung up first.

BFRB

Elizabeth Moore

She's like Gretel, but it's not breadcrumbs that fall from her hands. It's skin. It flakes off like snow; a trail of DNA leading the witch right to her. She picks and pulls and tears at every little catch of skin. Bloody hands. Scabs crust up, harden, as her fingernails dig, dig, dig. Bloody lips. Who could ever want to kiss her? Lipstick couldn't even cover the damage. Bloody mouth. The insides of her cheeks are shredded. But no one looks, no one stares. It's dry skin. Chapped lips. It's shame and excuses.

HANSEL & GRETEL

Bradley R. Strahan

Tripping through the electric forest
they've left complaints behind:
"too loud, too late, too dirty,
too…" two alone wandering
through the late afternoon music:
wind twanging in trees,
harsh metallic chorus of crows.

The sun suffers a short circuit.
As shadows flood the forest floor
Hansel tries to play his harmonica
but his mouth is too dry.
Gretel feels her guitar
and pack growing heavier.

Through twilit woods
a funky rhythm throbs.
It reels the wanderers in
gasping like fish to the surface
of a loud/bright clearing.

In the center, a small pavilion
framed by huge loudspeakers,
the grass dotted with

giant toadstools that hum
and sway with the waves of sound.

On stage, a freaky broad,
white hair to her waist,
lays down a solid beat
on a black iron kettle.
"That's bad!" "Kick Ass!" "Heavy"
the pair intone, already swaying
like blonde mushrooms.

The sound stops. The witch
fixes them with two black beads,
invites them to her pad. They follow
past tumbled toadstools.

A door beneath the stage opens
to single candle gleam.
Plastic bags hang from walls.
The hag offers hashish, coke…
Gretel puffs pure gold.
Hansel mellows out on hash.

The witch claims to be a promoter,
shows them her studio,
promises big bucks if they're tight
They audition, become her *backup band*.
"Better than a field of animated fungus,"
she mumbles behind their backs.

Each night they jam
getting ready for the big break.
Hansel flies higher and higher.
Gretel begins to doubt
as she watches beady eyes devour him.
She dreams of wolves,
smokes less and less.

Hansel wasted, the witch all smiles;
Gretel, cold sober, pretends.
Out comes the black kettle.
Up flares the magic flame,
Hansel dangerously near.
The witch prepares to push.

Gretel grabs her ax,
swings and lays the bitch
headfirst in her own broth.
Guitar shatters, fire scatters.
Gretel flees, Hansel stumbling after.

The *promoter* and her stash
go up in smoke.

MIRANDA MIRANDA

Brooke Wonders

My wife, Sycorax, has sewn witches into all my dresses.

We stand inside the walk-in closet we share, off the bedroom we share, inside the house we share, inside the life we share, but maybe wish we didn't. Sycorax shouts that I don't appreciate her labor. Her eyelids are tattooed with dancing Calibans I can see only when she blinks. I stroke them tenderly when we make love.

I examine each dress for faults. Queen Mab stitched into the bodice of my wedding gown. Lilith folded into the hem of my emerald sundress. The Sea Hag pinned to the shoulder of my best gray A-line, the one I wear to Appreciation Meetings at work. (I am an usher at the opera house.) I must commend my faultless wife—each witch has been precisely calibrated to appeal to base desires. I do not see Baba Yaga, though I look for her chicken legs and her cackle. We sold the baby clothes at a garage sale last summer. I peer into the darkest recesses. I fear I will never get these witches out of my wardrobe.

"Where have you put Ophelia? Where is Desdemona?" I ask. This makes my wife's wrath boil over, a cauldron of sea-snakes. "Where be Macbeth's witches three?"

Sycorax, not yet grown into a hoop, loved her Caliban. She carved his name into the heartwood where she imprisoned Ariel. She remembers how his fat baby fingers crushed sticks to sand. A sad stick bundle, a heartwood stick bundle, a bundle of blue sticks on a gray background. Despite what Prospero once believed, Caliban and I have nothing in common.

I take Sycorax's throat in my mouth to distract her. She latches sharp teeth onto my skin, tongue catching in my hair. We twine fingers together to make a net. I name her Beauty and Blame-Taker and Ouroboros, and she thrums back to me *Miranda, Miranda.*

I don't know why witches, but since the first day I found Baba Yaga cackling under the baby clothes and a sparkly Glinda inside the pocket of my yellow shiftdress, Sycorax and I have metamorphosed into she-monsters. We speak through touch, guttural growls, and taut silences. She grows more spherical day by day. I wrap my arms around the roundness of her.

A blue-eyed tempest lives inside the hump of her back. It threatens to overflow out her ears. Every night, I beat back the sea with a pair of oars. My earholes are forever wet.

Sycorax invites me out for sushi.

"Should we invite the witches?" I ask.

She exits the closet without me, which I guess means no. Sycorax takes a light coat off its hanger. She made this coat herself, crocheting together obedient sprites. I apologize to the witches and promise to bring home some leftover sushi, if there is any, because it doesn't keep long, so they might as well eat it. I follow Sycorax into the night like a bad dream.

At the sushi joint, Sycorax orders seaweed salad, which she braids into her hair. I order plain white rice, miso soup, and a Philadelphia roll to go. We don't discuss the witches. The man behind the counter slices fish oh-so-thinly. His bald head shines like eel sauce and his nametag reads PHIL STEIN. He's good with a knife. I watch his hands through the glass.

"Do you like working here?" Our eyes meet above a slab of uncut yellowtail.

"Where does the moon go when it rains?" he asks me.

I haven't the foggiest.

"Isn't it afraid of getting wet?" asks Sycorax. Her soy sauce has flowed over the rim of her plate. There is wasabi between her teeth and her hair smells like toasted sesame seeds and brine. She has never been more beautiful. The tempest inside her waxes and wanes.

"Are you a witch?" Sycorax asks Phil.

"Patrons have told me I'm bewitching." He rubs a hand across his bald head in slow circles. Sycorax can't stop watching. His hands drip sweat. He leans past the counter and holds out a sweaty palm. She picks up a piece of perfect tuna and swirls it across his skin. Eats it.

"Don't, it's raw," he says, but it's too late.

"Don't, it's raw," she whispers back, but he's already begun shoving whole sushi-grade salmon steaks down his throat until he chokes. Sycorax joins him at the cutting block. They eat with their hands. Their clutching sounds might be aggression or worship.

While they eat, I secure all the chopsticks, napkins, and sushi boats in the place. I fit each boat with a chopstick main mast and a napkin sail. I carry dental floss in my purse for just this occasion. Each ship gets a leash of floss. I pull my ships across the restaurant floor. The lives of a thousand tiny seamen depend on me. The tempest inside my wife howls for effect.

When there's no more fish left, Phil turns on the neon sign reading SORRY, WE'RE CLOSED. My hands tangle in the floss. My ships capsize.

"Then let's keep dancing," says Sycorax.

I examine my toes, which tap in time to the K-pop coming through the speakers. Phil busies himself with cleanup. In a sushi joint, everything must be carefully sterilized.

Outside the restaurant, two puddles hold one another and waltz under no moon. My father, Prospero, walks by, splashing. He carries a book. The tempest inside my wife ruffles its feathers.

"Listen," says Sycorax, "it's him or me."

My father has never sewn me a single witch. Not one of the witches I asked for. Prospero drops his book. It lands in a puddle. Phil scurries outside, muttering about littering, garbage scaring off the customers. Trash, trash.

"Give that here." Sycorax opens to page one. Inside, a pattern for a shirtwaist dress, the kind worn by working girls. The tempest inside her sings like the sea. The witches in my closet croon in answer, so loud I can hear them even in a sushi restaurant miles away. They creel their hunger.

"Give us a spell," says Phil.

"Patience," answers Sycorax. "Please," she says, "please." She's staring at me.

I find myself grown into a hoop. The tempest inside bursts free. The witches in my wardrobe run off with all my best ghosts. I miss ushering in my dresses. I'd forgotten all about the gray silk I wore to *Tosca,* the red velvet I wore to *Figaro,* the purple brocade I wore to *Don Giovanni.* Prospero's long robes shush over the horizon. The moon comes out, and it begins to rain. Sycorax waltzes with Phil while the puddles applaud winningly. I roll myself in circles around them as they dance, mouths at each other's throats.

"Where are you going?" I ask.

Witches flutter down from the heavens. They swarm around us. The Evil Queen steps into me like a ballgown. She likes me better than a mirror. The tempest curls itself up and closes its eyes. It's naked and answers to no one. Prospero is much too far away to hear me call for help.

I never see my wife again.

In the morning, all her things are gone. Sycorax has left a note. *Miranda, Miranda, my best witch, my moon. You could say sorry, but it wouldn't change a thing.*

The tempest is Ariel in the heartwood screaming for release. It is made up of obedient sprites. It was never meant for witches. On the backside of her note, a pattern for a light coat, perfect to ward off rain.

IN SICKNESS, HEALTH, AND SPACE-TIME

Brianna Noll

> The fourth; the dimension of stillness.
> And the power over wild beasts.
> – Ezra Pound, Canto 49

Born the same day, less
than an hour apart, the lovers
ask each other, *Are you me?*

The universal ancestor of all
life on earth was only half alive,
and yet here we are, alike and thrumming.

The lovers love papercraft, love
turning two dimensions into three
and dream of four, of tesseracts

and helical tesseracts somehow,
impossibly, unspooling. Imagine how
DNA would evolve in the fourth dimension.

I bet you can't. I know the lovers
can't, yet they wish to dabble with time,
even if it threatens their shared identity.

They're willing to sacrifice
incidentals if it means they might
turn a paper cake into something greater,

puzzling and intangible, like pure
form. How does another dimension affect
a relationship? The empath can tell you

what connection feels like, and
it's directional: a magnetic field, a strand
of nucleic acid. We are and are

not one. We are and are not
two. The lovers love to imagine all
the possibilities they will and will not be.

PARTITIONED SPACE

Brianna Noll

The galaxy makes a monarch of the sky,
purpled and gilded. In an overpopulated
universe, only kings are sanctuaries.

In the bedroom of a ballerina, gauzy
curtains snag the crumbling brick across
the narrow alley, fray and string.

Orion the Hunter stalks a perfect sky,
no nebula for camouflage. The bears
are unmoving, or moving like clockwork.

The ballerina's room is just a space,
like all other spaces, in which to move.
Even breathing she's an artist sculpting time.

In gravity's rainbow there's a point
where time does not exist, where space
does not exist. There are no black holes there.

Celestial light is history, and the ballerina
can't see the stars. If her only memory is muscle
memory, she might be empress of the ever-present.

SURVIVING LINEAR TIME

Brianna Noll

We've been dying
since the day we met,
but at least the dying's
slow, unlike the gingko:
in mere hours, it sheds
an impressionist ocean
of gold on the lawn.
Is the future ahead of us
or below? We've become
animals who can't flourish
because we know
we're in decline. The best
we can manage is to grind
gingko leaves, mix them
with talc, and cover
our hands in the powder
so we can leave a trace
of ourselves on everything
we touch. Follow the golden
smudges: you'll see
around each of us
parabolas or the rings
of a target—we are fixed
points around which
the world is drawn.

MISSIVE ON AN OLD REFUTATION OF TIME

Joachim Glage

There is a town in northernmost Japan that is so close to the eastern extremity of Russia—the Russian-controlled Kunashir Island is not even twenty miles off—the street signs there are all written in both Japanese and Cyrillic. It is a cold and windy little place, sparsely populated; lots of snow in the wintertime. Near the shore there stands a small striped lighthouse and a row of calm-faced statues that gaze out over the water (a monument, I recently learned, to the *bushi* who, according to lore, defended an Ainu fishing village from marauders some four centuries ago). On clear days (even the most frigid) the sun bounces and gleams warmly off of the Nemuro Strait. I dream of living there, in that strange overlapping of Russia and Japan. I dream of the quiet snow, of the uneventful neighborhoods and the oft-unpeopled streets, and of the warmly-lit tea shop and bodega that I've seen in a photograph. I dream of the Japanese and Russian street signs—some of them warnings, no doubt—which, to me, would stand only for meaningless, melodious sounds.

Less frequent, but not less aglow in my dreams, is the village of Dalvik in Iceland—a satellite, so to speak, of the Lesser Grímsvötn volcano near the western edge of the Vatnajökull ice cap. The volcano, which smolders beneath clouds veined with its ash (though it has not technically erupted in over three-hundred years), is something of a geological oddity; it is the only properly columnar, sub-glacial volcano in the northern hemisphere that exhibits signs of carbon-based magma. Its uppermost peak juts strangely from the ice, bare of snow, like an obelisk. The village of Dalvik, really little more than an outpost, and located just outside the glacier's edge some forty kilometers west of the volcano, was established gradually between 1959 and 1962 in order to service the geologists who came from all over the world to study that strange anomaly of the earth. As one might guess, the village is not exactly a concentrated geographical entity; it exists in small pockets of activity here and there, and parts of it move from place to place, depending upon the season and funding from universities. Several leagues to the west of the glacier is the sparsely-furnished Denmark Hotel, often taken to be the western boundary of Dalvik (and probably the only place within fifty kilometers where one can get a good hot shower); closer are the various chalets, quickly erected and then torn down again, where food is served, supplies are sold, and expeditions are planned. Near the start of the glacier one may find the drab tent where sleeps Rúrik Sigþórsson, the lone guide who earns his humble living showing scientists and tourists the best routes up the slopes of the volcano (and even into her mouth), and whose throbbing face, splotched like a rancid cheese and red as a sockeye, flakes freely from lip and chin. I've dreamed of being bundled up in Rúrik Sigþórsson's tent; I've had visions of my own ruined face, reddened and marked by the alternating extremes of heat and cold. I've dreamed of succeeding good Rúrik, of taking his place.

I've dreamed, also, of a street corner somewhere in the outskirts of Buenos Aires, written about by Borges in a short text called "Feeling in Death." This text is of singular importance to scholars and lovers of Borges's work, for it is the only one that he reproduced on at least three occasions: first in his youthful book, *The Language of the Argentines,* and then again in his 1936 essay "A History of Eternity," and then again in "A New Refutation of Time" from 1947 (a revision, somewhat, of the 1936 essay). The text recounts an experience Borges had while out for a walk one evening. He arrives at a corner in one of the barrios of Buenos Aires, a neighborhood vaguely familiar to him, but also mysterious; he is struck by the beauty of the place, the simple houses, the red pink sky like a wall, colors that exude tenderness, the "street of elemental clay." This perception of a scene both ordinary and picturesque then yields, as often happens in Borges, to metaphysical speculation:

> "I stood looking at that simple scene. I thought, no doubt aloud: 'This is the same as it was thirty years ago...' [...] That pure representation of homogeneous facts—calm night, limpid wall, rural scent of honeysuckle, elemental clay—is not merely identical to the scene on that corner so many years ago; it is, without similarities or repetitions, the same. If we can intuit that sameness, time is a delusion..."

Borges does not specify the name of the street, or the barrio in which that corner was located. I think it must have been in Palermo, but of course this would be the Palermo of a hundred years ago, and perhaps even further back in time than that: the Palermo of Borges's dreams (a Palermo when the Maldonado was still a freely flowing stream, and knife-wielding hoodlums strutted and flaunted themselves, or else hid in the half-darkness of doorways, and certain poor neighborhoods were only a stroll from stench-filled stockyards and all-but impassable marshes). I too have dreamed of these old outskirts of Buenos Aires, and I've dreamed also of modern-day Barracas and of now-chic Palermo; I wonder if, in spite of their many changes, I could still somehow find the exact spot where Borges once stood and saw into eternity. Or, if I should fail at that, but if I nonetheless walked aimlessly enough, and if I took just the right careless turn around just the right Argentine corner, and if I saw the early-evening salmon sky, and beneath it a simple one-story home, and if I felt the life there, and the tenderness, and smelled the honeysuckle and the fig trees, and spied an indignant cactus growing from a masonry jar in the corner of a doorway, then might I too become convinced, even if only later in a memory, of the illusoriness of time?

I think the half-existence of these places, their degree of unreality (Borges himself uses this word, *irrealidad*), is what draws me to them. More than other places, it seems to me, they exist inside the fleeting present, and only there. Once they are gone, no historian will ever think to mention them. In this quality we are, perhaps, the same.

Tomorrow our platoon is being sent back to the trenches. They tell us the third division is holding ground, but we know better. The GR outfit has been stretched thin. I hope this letter finds its way to you, and finds you well, my dear mother. Thank you for the books. As you can see, I've put them to good use already.

TREE ENVY

Lierin Woods

I talked to a tree today.
She was achy, she said, she was flaked.
I craned my neck to reach my own boughs,
though while hers were up, mine were down.
They say when knots form, it's stress.
Hers were many, but worn. I asked,
"What stresses could a tree form?"
She waved at me in green ivy.
I've felt the weight of a billion
wings, the legs of a thousand arachnids,
webbing me. I've knelt in the grove
for a century, stealing the air
and giving it back fresher.
I've shed for the betterment
of flowers, grasses, and greens.
And I can see all around,
even be all around, rooting,
shifting, a foundation of me.
This is but a form of freedom.
I lay back listening. These,
like a dream a soldier dreams,
wandering miseries. I can't be
shadowed with bottomed boughs.
Envy's eyes looked into me.
This is but a form of freedom.

THE STORM-KING AND THE TREE BELOW

Gregor Southard

Overhead,
the Storm-King rumbled,
"I am arriving soon and you
can't stop me."

The tree below
desperately
trying to bud,
replied, "I've been waiting
for you."

The Storm-King,
he paused, and the wind relaxed.
"Are you quite sure?"
The tree below,
she answered,
"I am in the pangs of birth,
but my leaves,
they're too dry to push out."

The Storm-King smiled,
his light shining through
his dark gray and blue coat,
simply said,

"Why do you think
I blew in just now?"

The tree below,
she simply smiled
and stretched out her limbs, saying
"You may proceed, sir."

A ROOM ALONE WITH BIRDS

K. Branagan

Medium: Mixed media — Acrylic, ink, paper, textile, and metal on wood panel

Dimensions: 24"x 24"

AIN'T NO VIRGIN ON THE ROCKS

K. Branagan

Medium: Acrylic and ink on wood panel

Dimensions: 36"x 48"

SHE DANCES WITH DEATH
K. Branagan
Medium: Acrylic on canvas
Dimensions: 20”x16”

GUITAR
Evan McHenry
Medium: Photography
Dimensions: 30"x20"

UNTITLED #4
Jeremy Szuder
Medium: Ink on Paper
Dimensions: 8"x10"

UNTITLED #7

Jeremy Szuder

Medium: Ink on Paper

Dimensions: 5"x7"

UNTITLED #18
Jeremy Szuder
Medium: Ink and Watercolor on Paper
Dimensions: 9”x12”

THE TOMB AND THE DOOR
Sonnet Mondal
Medium: Digital
Dimensions: 3000x3750

BOOK SIGNINGS

Gregor Southard

"You have to be seen," they say.
So, I drive from bookstore to bookstore,
trying to convince the pleasant
yet indifferent bookstore managers
to let me set up shop.
"Email me."
"Call me in two weeks."
"I'll look the book over."
"We don't normally host poets."
"Maybe in April?" I offer.
That's National Poetry Month, you know!

The price of gas
is no friend to a poet.
And, by the way,
songwriters are not poets.
They're songwriters.
No shame in that distinction
just more money (and girls).

Two weeks later,
the email does come,
and I'm signed on
for some Sunday in April.

Convenient.

Book signings are fun
because getting a person
to stop at your table
is like trying to talk to a girl
when Keith Urban is in the room.

So, they stroll on by
tilting their heads away,
speeding up or trying
to read a sign
advertising the latest John Grisham novel
on the far side of the store.
But some people do stop by,
that's what friends are for.

DEB SANDERS'S ETCH A SKETCHES

Michael Martone

It was *the* Christmas present to have in 1960. I was five, and the next Christmas I used it to write Santa a note and left it there next to the plate of cookies and the carrots for the reindeer. That was the last year I believed. The cookies were gone and carrots half-eaten and my message all erased and Santa, or someone I was supposed to believe was Santa, made an attempt to write something back, the lines like cracks in the glass. Years have gone by. I stopped writing notes. I stopped drawing the pictures, all scratchy and nervous lines slipping off at odd angles when my fingers slipped on the dials. I've spent years, finally, going back and forth, back and forth, up and down, rubbing away the silver coating line by line, revealing, as the dust sifted away, the elegant mechanism beneath the metallic film, the stylus and the articulated beams, cables, and springs. Every time the apparatus appeared (and there were many times, I bought new ones after I erased the old ones), I was always surprised that the magic that seemed so evident before us could be so patently peeled away. I've hung the transparent shells now on the walls around my windows, windows framed by windows. In the winter, the glass frosts over, and I find I take my finger and touch the cold, a kind of cursor, and melting away the cataract of ice, a little peephole there and then another, that then expands as my finger etches out a horizontal streak across a pane, exposing the predictable geometry of wintery Winesburg beyond. It passes the time.

JIM O'DAY'S FOLLY

Michael Martone

If anyone ever wants to build anything again here in Winesburg, I'm ready. But no one has wanted to build anything in a long time, so I wait. I wait, tools at the ready. I have all the materials I need to build the building's building structures—the scaffolding and the forms, the struts and braces. They fit together neatly to build towers and the skeletons of walls, and they come apart just as neatly, back into their piles of tubes and joints and platforms and turnbuckles. I wait for the phone to ring. It never rings. I spend my time constructing and tearing down my elaborate skeletons of scaffold. Architects would call these follies—buildings that are built for no other reason than to build them. They are brand new fake ruins, fun to look at, but in no way habitable. Though you will see me living up there, I guess, bolting over the monkey bars, this jungle gym. Every day, I rig a more and more elaborate maze of beams and pipes, cross-braced and buttressed—a building made out of the methods of building buildings. And each night, I take it apart, revealing, once this facade of a facade is torn down, the nothing I was constructing out of the nothing all around me.

MY GRANDFATHER'S HOG OILER

Michael Martone

There aren't that many left. Most were gathered up during the war, scrapped for the cast iron, now probably distributed as shrapnel all over Europe and the Pacific islands. Granddad came home from that war and took the GI Bill money and put it into a farm, 80 acres, outside Winesburg. He used to say he "played" with hogs, farrowed and finished. I think I remember that place. I remember the smell that Granddad always said was "the smell of money." The hogs were spooky. They would look at you the way a human would. And they always were escaping out of each and every more elaborate pen Granddad would, my dad would say, construct. "He was leaking pigs," Dad would say. I remember visiting after the family moved to town. The yards and pens a wreck with rusting tools and implements, old seed drills and steel wheeled harrows. There were lumps and chunks of metal the edges worn smooth where the hogs rubbed and rooted against and around them. I lugged home this souvenir, an old oiler I found mired near the busted troughs. The drums still roll and turn, but the life is all worn out of it, a curiosity, a conversation starter now that I keep in the front room. "What the hell is that?" I hope someone will say when that someone visits. But no one visits. I sit in the parlor and worry the old useless device that warms, sooner or later, to my touch.

FALLING

Michael Buckius

Is it true
that for every person
   falling in love
   there is a person
   falling out of love
And for every person
getting into their car
   there is a person
   falling out of their car

Learning how to get out of a car
is a rite of passage
for many teenagers

This world may seem silly
and full of injury
because it is

Sometimes when people get older
they take the keys
and return home with groceries
Sometimes they take the keys
and return home
different people

SQUAB

James Tadd Adcox

For weeks, a pair of mourning doves traded off tending a nest haphazardly constructed above the door to our balcony. You felt a closeness to them, you said; it was a good omen. There had been a scare at the beginning of your pregnancy, but now the sonograms showed a boy who the doctor assured us looked healthy. If the doves were afraid of us, they didn't show it. Mornings, you would step out on the balcony and say hello while you had your coffee; and once a week I built a fire on the small grill we kept there and cooked burgers or sausages, one eye on the doves all the while, worried at first that my presence might drive them away. One day you called me out to show me the doves, together in their nest, warming the awkward bodies of two newborn squabs: small, alien things, skulls too apparent beneath the heads, feathers in disarray. We thought of them as neighbors. Then, two days after the squabs appeared, a thumping and beating outside our backdoor: I looked out to see a blue jay near the edge of the balcony and a small body flapping ineffectually beside him. He had pulled down one of the squabs; a dove stood several feet away, looking on dumbly, while the blue jay attacked his child, pecking at its neck. We watched all this from the window. When the jay carried the small corpse off with him, you said, "At least we won't have to clean it up."

Afterwards, we found all three of them—the two adult doves and the remaining squab—in the place where the blue jay had butchered the squab. The remaining squab, too young to have flown down himself (and who, we concluded, must have been knocked down during the attack), perched between the adults, who pecked at the feathers on each other's necks—perhaps grooming each other, perhaps comforting. I could not help seeing a bloodless reenactment of the violence that had occurred in this same place less than an hour before. We left them alone. When we next came out to the porch, we found the tattered twigs of the nest, knocked from its place above the door; but no signs of the doves themselves, or the squab who was almost certainly too young to have flown away.

VAN GOGH ON SUICIDE PREVENTION

Hollie Dugas

In place of blood: flowers—slathered
across canvas as many years as you can
stomach. And this is important: Do not
discharge that 7mm Lefaucheux revolver,
shoot what's inside of you out onto golden
wheat. Instead, spread yourself forcefully
into the flora. And how much like a bloom
you are. I have witnessed the slightly wilted
iris crying joyously for his life. I give you
this iris—scatter yourself thick inside it.
There is solace in flowers, sweet release
in a symphony of color. Leave me
to the mutant sunflower—my calyx
of yellow flame, my burning halo.

FOOD FOR THOUGHT

James Rogers

Gerry turned on the TV in time to see the first pitch out at Citi Field. He settled into the armchair, a can of beer in his hand. He was looking forward to a relaxing evening and perhaps even a Mets win.

By the end of the first inning the Mets had given up two runs, left a man on third, and Gerry's wife had completed her ablutions. The bathroom door opened and Agnes stomped down the stairs, timbers creaking like a sailboat in heavy seas. "I thought you were doing the hedges?" she said.

"I'll do them tomorrow," Gerry answered as he lifted the can to his lips.

"That's what you said yesterday."

Gerry focused on the TV and tried to ignore her. But out of the corner of his eye he could see her plant her hand on her hip, a sure sign she was close to the boil.

"They're a disgrace," she continued. "Gerry! You said you'd do them."

Gerry threw his arms up. "Alright, alright! Just let me finish my beer."

He got the hedge cutters from the basement and started with the hedge on the left, working his way clockwise. The steel blades sliced through the branches with ease. About twenty minutes into the job, he spotted the dead cat, under the fir tree. He approached it with interest, until he saw it was a skinny old stray, a bag of bones. He wondered what to do with it. If Agnes caught sight of it, she'd freak out. She hated cats, felt like they were watching her, stalking her, waiting for her to … what? Stumble? "I've never seen a cat smile," she said once. Gerry had wanted to laugh.

He couldn't understand her revulsion. They were just animals, like any other. They lived for the sake of living. In his own way, he was doing his best to help her see that. It was slow work, but he was confident he would succeed in the end. In the meantime, he made sure to keep her garden and her life free of live specimens.

Dead ones? They were a different story. Gerry decided to leave this one be. Let the maggots have it. With a bit of luck, Agnes would never see it. He continued with the hedges.

Another hour saw the job done, apart from sweeping up. Gerry stepped back and admired his handiwork. "I suppose she was right," he whispered. "They were a disgrace."

He got the rake and the broom and filled three garbage bags with the clippings, but left a scattering of twigs and leaves over the dead cat. He hefted two bags out to the curb. On his way back for the third he found Agnes on inspection duty. "You missed a bit," she said as she picked up the rake.

"Leave it!" Gerry shouted. He darted across the garden, but wasn't fast enough. Agnes pulled at the pile of twigs and leaves, saw the cat, and started screaming.

"Oh my God!" She dropped the rake and clutched her face. "Oh my God!"

"Ssh, will you. Ssh!"

She spun on one foot like a top-heavy ballerina. "Oh my God!" she cried again as she ran for the house.

Gerry sighed. There was no chance now of leaving the cat to rot. Agnes wouldn't sleep till it was gone.

It was a sickeningly delicate operation. He spread a garbage bag out on the grass, then rolled the cat onto it using the hedge cutters. Three legs and the head parted company with the body. The stench of decay filled Gerry's nostrils and his mouth filled with bile. Screwing up his face, he used the cutters like enormous tweezers and lifted the legs onto the plastic. The head was trickier; not all the insides came with the skull and the eyes tumbled through their sockets. He dropped the lot onto the plastic and turned away, almost vomiting.

He stood with his hands on his hips, fortifying himself with deep breaths. The spinning eyes kept falling before his own, over and over. He was reminded of *Itchy and Scratchy* from *The Simpsons*.

He swallowed several times, trying to get rid of the taste in his mouth. After one more mighty chest expansion, he returned to the task. He placed another garbage bag on top of the first, then slid the cat sandwich inside a third. The image made him giggle and retch at the same time.

“Is it gone?” Agnes asked. She was huddled in the corner of the sofa. The TV was on, but she was hardly watching it. Its light played upon her in the growing darkness, lending her a shiver. Gerry’s heart tightened. He didn’t like to see her this way. He sat down and tried to get his arm around her but could only reach the crook of her neck. She was rigid. “Calm down. It’s alright. It’s done.”

“What did you do with it?”

“I threw it in the garbage can.”

She leaped from the sofa like an astronaut on the moon. “No, no, no! You have to get rid of it!” She stared out the window at the galvanized can, her eyes bulging so much Gerry thought they might tumble out, like the cat’s. “Get it out of here!”

“Where?”

“Anywhere. The garbage can too. Oh God.” She shuddered, ran up the stairs, slammed the bathroom door and locked it.

What to do? Gerry stood on the sidewalk and surveyed the scene. The innocent looking garbage can sat against a utility pole, the bags of clippings beside it. Two posters for missing cats were pinned to the pole. He’d tear them down if he thought he’d get away with it, mostly because they were a torment for poor Agnes. Every morning as she went off to work, she had to avert her eyes. Where everyone else saw sad little fur balls, Agnes saw demons with eyes that burrowed through to her soul and gleefully counted her remaining days.

Ailurophobia, it was called. He’d looked it up, after she’d refused to get out of the car because a meaty specimen was sitting on the neighbor’s wall, staring at them. Wikipedia said treatment required a psychiatrist. Agnes wouldn’t hear of that. Psychiatrists were only for people with something wrong with them. Gerry knew full well there was no point in arguing. He’d decided subtlety was the key. Sneak the medicine in, like you would with a child. There were little or no indications yet that his efforts would be rewarded, but he wasn’t about to give up. He kept reminding himself it would take time.

Gerry put the garbage can on the back seat of the car and drove to the rear of the supermarket, where people deposit the bottles and cans. There was no one around at that time of the evening. He set the bin down in the corner, its handles clanking loudly in the quiet of the evening.

When he got back to the house the streetlights were on. He went into the garden for the last bag of clippings. In the semidarkness he could just make out a shape lying next to the bag. He walked over and put his hands on his hips. "Bloody hell." Another dead cat. He nudged it with his foot. A much healthier looking specimen this time. Well, at least it was before it died.

He looked up at his bedroom window, half expecting to see Agnes. But there was no sign of her. The curtains were drawn and she was most likely wrapped up in the blankets, desperately trying to sleep.

He tore another garbage bag from the roll and quickly packaged the second kitty. The garbage men would have this one and Agnes would know nothing of it. "No telling what killed you," he whispered as he lifted the bag and turned for the street.

The woman from next door was standing behind him. "Jesus Christ, Eva! You scared the shit out of me."

"Do you have to use such language, Gerry?" Eva said. In the artificial light she looked more emaciated than usual. Gerry was reminded of *The Scream*.

"Sorry. It's just you gave me a fright."

"Have you seen Snowball?"

"Snowball?"

"Mrs. Vitelli's cat. White with one black ear. She's been missing for … well, it must be a week now."

Gerry shook his head. "No, haven't seen her."

"A lot of cats have gone missing. I saw a video on YouTube about foxes roaming the city at night. Can you believe that? Do you think a fox would take a cat?"

"I wouldn't have a clue."

"I think it might." She looked about the garden. "You did a nice job on the hedges."

"It was about time."

Gerry sighed inwardly as Eva turned to go. He was relieved that this mad day was coming to an end and he was looking forward to a little TV, a few more beers.

After he'd checked on Agnes, of course.

The bag twitched. "Fucking hell!"

"Gerry!"

The bag thrashed and mewed. Gerry dropped it and Eva jumped as a four-legged Lazarus shot out of the plastic like death wouldn't catch him twice.

"That's Jimmy Willie," Eva gasped. "Mrs. Krupnick's cat." She stared at Gerry.

"Jimmy Willie?" Gerry giggled. Eva backed away.

The moon was high and Jimmy Willie was on the prowl, none the worse for his sojourn in the body bag. The mouse scampered and squealed as Jimmy Willie pounced, his claws extended and his heart thumping in anticipation of crunching bones and warm oozing blood and tender muscle. A lump hammer caught him on the back of the head. His legs went from under him, his jaw hit the concrete.

"There," Gerry whispered. "Now we know what killed you."

It was almost noon on Sunday morning when Gerry yawned his way down the stairs. He could hear Agnes sloshing about in the bathroom and he figured it was time to start making her breakfast. Tea and toast and an omelet.

The omelet was sizzling nicely when the doorbell rang. Gerry frowned as he turned off the gas and walked over to the door, spatula in hand. Who would be calling this early on a Sunday? He opened the door to find Mrs. Krupnick on the porch, her round face pale, her eyes wide. "Eva says you had Jimmy Willie!"

Gerry stared at her. "Your cat?" he said. "I don't know where he is."

"She said you had him on Friday."

"He comes in and out of my garden."

"She said you had him in a bag."

"I thought he was dead."

Mrs. Krupnick put her hands to her face and wailed.

"Calm down. I said I thought he was dead. But he upped and ran off."

Eva came out her front door and joined the party on the porch. Mrs. Krupnick turned to her. "I can't find Jimmy Willie."

Eva stared at Gerry. "Are you stealing cats, Gerry?"

"Stealing cats! Are you gone daft? What would I be stealing cats for?"

"I don't know. But you had Jimmy Willie in a bag."

"My Jimmy Willie."

"I thought he was dead," Gerry reiterated. "But he ran off. You saw him."

Eva's mouth twisted. "You thought he was dead?" she sneered.

"Yes. Now for goodness sake, will you let me go. Here I am, trying to make breakfast and you come about the place with nonsense talk about dead cats." He tried to close the door, but Eva pushed it back against him.

"Dead cats?" she said.

"Dead cats, live cats, they're nothing to do with me."

"But why would you say dead?"

"For Christ's sake, Eva, will you leave me alone!"

"And there's that language again."

"Oh so what about my language! What do you expect when you come here with your crazy accusations!" He could feel himself slipping as quickly as his voice was rising and he didn't like it. He tried again to close the door, but Eva put her shoulder to it this time. "Get the hell away from my door!" he shouted.

A police car stopped in front of his driveway. Gerry couldn't believe it: the cops, just when you need them. "Officers!" he shouted as two uniformed police officers got out of the car. He wondered how they'd managed to spot the altercation. That is until one of them opened the trunk and pulled out his garbage can.

Gerry's eyes opened wide and his heart stuttered. Eva and Mrs. Krupnick watched the male officer carry the can up the path to the porch. They both took a step to one side, distancing themselves from the situation.

"This your garbage can, sir?" asked the female officer. Her partner turned the bin to display the bottom and the address written there in neat letters. Gerry had forgotten about the address. Damn Agnes! Did she really think someone would steal their bin? He'd laughed at the time, wondering how the printed address was supposed to prevent such larceny.

Gerry decided to brazen it out. "It is indeed," he said in mock surprise. "Where did you find it?"

"There was a dead cat inside," the cop continued.

That started Mrs. Krupnick off again. She rose in pitch like an air-raid siren. "Jimmy Willie!"

"It wasn't Jimmy Willie," Gerry said. "It was an old stray cat."

"So you put the dead cat in here?"

"Yeah. And then someone stole the bin."

"Why would someone steal your bin, sir?"

"I have no idea."

"He's been kidnapping other cats," Eva said.

"Kidnapping?"

"Yes. He put a live one in a bag. I saw him."

"Sir?"

"For God's sake, how many times do I have to say it? I thought it was dead! Officers, can you please ask these women to leave? They're on my property, accusing me of the most ridiculous things."

"But what about my Jimmy Willie?"

"Oh you and your goddam Jimmy Willie!" Gerry shouted, his hands flying. The spatula arced, catapulting half-cooked omelet. A morsel of meat landed on Mrs. Krupnick's cheek. Gerry stared at it. He clamped his mouth shut but not before a giggle escaped from between his teeth. Four sets of eyes stared at him.

"Gerry!" came a shout from above, shattering the moment. "Why is there a police car outside?"

Agnes took care of them. No better woman. She had the pair of women scampering away in seconds. Even the cops seemed a bit intimidated, even though she thanked them for returning the garbage can, while casually pointing out to Gerry how right she'd been to put their address on it.

Gerry was impressed. Not with her efficient evacuation of the porch, but with the way she convinced the others that she really was pleased by the return of the bin. He would almost have believed her himself if it hadn't been for the way she kept twisting her hands together. He wondered if it was the first sign of progress. If it had happened a month earlier Gerry was sure she'd have shot back up the stairs at the sight of that oversized cat-casket, even at the expense of embarrassing herself in front of the neighbors.

Gerry went back to the stove and the omelet while Agnes closed the door. He smiled thinly as he turned on the gas and poked at the onions and peppers and the little bits of meat.

Agnes sat down at the table to the sound of the sizzling pan. "They were treating me like I was a lunatic," Gerry said as he flipped the omelet. "Like I was the mad one."

He turned off the gas, slid the omelet onto a plate and landed it in front of Agnes. She picked up the fork, cut off a chunk and popped it into her mouth. Gerry turned away. "I thought we were out of chicken," Agnes said.

Gerry thought of the little fridge in the basement, the one Agnes never went near. "No," he said, "I restocked." A picture of Mrs. Krupnick and the tiny morsel of Jimmy Willie on her cheek popped into his head. He smiled, but only for a moment. He could hear Agnes chew, swallow. He turned around again and forced himself to watch her eat. He knew it wasn't nice, what he was doing to his wife, and he took no pleasure in it. But medicine was seldom nice.

THE SUN AND THE MARSH PLAYED STRATEGY GAMES

Ryan Bollenbach

After the mysterious birth
Of the wilds
The sun and marsh
Split their days
Playing Go

Between every game
They took a minute
To get to know each other
Saying nothing and asking the other
How they got here

Weather became
As they learned their strategies
And the marsh's vines grew
Toward sun's thighs

On the millionth game
Thunder struck
Bacteria came in
And in the hum
Of the first infection
They each felt the other's true name

THE SUN AS A CHILD

Ryan Bollenbach

In the hot daylight the hares speak about the sun as a child
How he waddled in his small shoes of yellow leather
Cried because he thought the loam
Would keep his heat forever

He pointed his round, gaseous fingers
At the river and said river
Pointed at the armpit of the gulf
And said boiling to release kinetic energy

As a boy he hugged everything   Trees   Trash
White glinting teeth of the bobcat prowling

Mourned every farting out into nothing
After a second in his clutch

"We made fun of him then,"
The hares said, "because we had already grown into our stoic futures
Came back a new species then died
Hundreds of times before he outgrew his cradle."

He asked them if they knew his friend Icarus
"It had been a long time since we'd seen him.
We have some bad news…."

They said from inside the shade of a dark wet dark cave
Just as they started to break the news
The wolf bit down

A GIANT IS ALWAYS INTERRUPTING: GIANT BERNARD'S NAME HAS CHANGED TO PROTECT HIS PAST

Brian Oliu

You came back to us changed, as many do when they disappear into the oceans—even though you are on the other side of the world, the world does not stop without you; you, you are of this world whether you wish to be or not. They never mentioned your name until it was too late—a white man with kanji written down the side of your face, meticulously painted on before every street fight or shouting match where you pretend to have lost the language of your birth; of how to say *champion,* of how to say *mine.* When we are tired, we drop the act—like any good giant, you end up dancing; how funny it is to see a body like that move, your thick Atlantic accent reappearing as you forget what was once forgotten. Giants have no choice but to be made up of a sum of their parts, so I believe that you were in there all along, friend. When you are larger than the mountain that bears your name, it is foolish to think you can be everything you wish to be at once.

FALLING AMONG CROWS

Anna E. Childs

As she lies by the pool, the legs of my younger sister stretch forward in the mottled sun.

Knowledge sets in. Entwined razor blade scars: her ankles tell a story thicker than my own.

Hot sky above the pool full and gray; crows soar black against it.

They have been everywhere this summer, atop the house, in every tree.

From above, rain appears to them as bullets, shining, beautiful as tears.

Here, June rain shimmers on pool surface, released by swollen underbelly of drops.

Seeing crows, I think of things proceeding on, and on; and on again.

There always is that animal dead beside the road, flesh exposed, eternal red carrion.

There are people who have it much worse than you, my husband says, eyes black

as crows' wings, and in them, something expands, fills up, black carbonation.

One month ago, it seemed the whole world must know, so swollen were my breasts, the

afternoon skies, as I prayed to suck life from crows' cries to
the dead cells within my womb.

My sister exhales, cigarette smoke rising softly upward, to crows and clouds.

Above, crows observe smoke, bullet rain, all the blood in the world, glisten of guts on the ground.

There are those who have been through the Unimaginable, my husband tells me,

yet he does not choke on black feathers deep within his throat.

Another crow flies overhead and clouds and rain speed by; day will soon be gone.

By the pool, sucking strength from summer, my younger sister with her cuts is as world weary as I.

Tallied by lines—red, white, pink—my sister's ankles whisper of bitterness bled,

of what is open, carrion washed by pellets of rain, etched, scarred with blood and dirt thick.

PHANTASMAGORIC TRUTH

Anna E. Childs

In the dark, after you lie spent, sleeping beside me, unaware that I still lie awake,
she visits our room. At times she appears at the foot of the bed, and she is white,
immaterial;

I am drawn to her as to a glow-worm or a will-of-the wisp; then she is in that corner

by your dresser—shining blue, as if under black light, her body filmy against oak brown.

Yet she never was under flashing lights with you; she did not move her body through smoke

of nightclubs to the devil's beat, and she certainly did not let peppermint Schnapps flow

across her teeth and throat and breasts, and then, burning, let your tongue run over her.

Still, there are so many times she flickers here, and I watch, unblinking, as you snore.

I must take the blame; I kneaded her from dank earth that summer night you took me

on wet grass; I wove her husk of blonde hair and the dingy shadows of her face asking you

if you had ever been in love. She came out from the blossoms of the honeysuckle and choked

the rose bushes, left her scent in every hair of my nostrils, and what can I say to finally make her go?

At three in the morning I reason with myself that she could be dead; she could be fat,

blonde hair short and gray. She could be drunk, her body stretched and loose from bearing

children;

she could be inoculating orphans in the third world, taking a scalpel to someone's chest.

Wherever she exists, she no longer rests in that picture you keep in the plastic box, beneath play programs and song lyrics; she no longer wears the raspberry colored prom dress,

standing just beside you, honeysuckles crisscrossing the fake floral backdrop behind.

From the night my hands clawed muddy earth beneath you, she moved from your heart to mine,

reaching with cold fingers to draw me through the forest, loam and leaves beneath our feet.

She waits just there, at the closet door; if you would open your eyes you would see her

pull me through to abject wilderness; there is no *shem* with which to choke her; she will never

leave.

When you turn to me, eyes closed, dreams overtaking you, and run your hand across my bare

breasts, she watches in the night, reflecting in blue eyes the theft of what was hers.

THICKETS

Anna E. Childs

Chaos of bracken here, briars bent over and round each other,
weeds head high, grain stalks that appear useful for bread,
yet scorch in sun, turn to fluff, drop, fade.
The ornately scalloped edges of poison leaves, green tinged with red,
the snakes moving through, the wild carrot flowers
elevated in regality, their centers of black onyx, just at my crown,
the sumac, rouged to heartrending sweetness, the blue and pink of morning glory.

Every week we seek out the blackberries, my husband, sons, and I,
reach back into winding riot of green and thorns
grasp for one shining cluster of sense,
for bulbs of black order forming together and hanging hidden if we only search and reach.

I look above at a whipping storm moving in and there are my boys, six and nine, knee-deep in

bracken, bare legs and arms exposed, and they, who still scream in pain at getting hurt, they

reach far back where our human limbs struggle to go, interweave their little fingers with the

thorns, seeking, seeking.

"There is something calming about this," my husband says to me, and there is, when each

morning there is dread to put feet on the floor and descend the stairs and make the coffee.

I sometimes dream of the thickets, the whole chaotic world of perfect, perfect sense, where if

there is light and heat and rain, berries grow; where if there are birds,

they eat; where if there are snakes, they crawl, where each wild thing willingly answers

the daily call to rise and unfurl and bake and swell and ripen and dry and fade and die.

Hell, this afternoon I know that the deer have stood on this same beaten patch of grass

where my feet rest; I can smell their piss as I reach, reach, farther, back and beyond and behind,

the black orbs hanging, just there—can you see them? Can you not see into these other worlds?

Thunder, spats of rain as quarters on the pavement of the road we stand beside.
One son falls and cries. Wind whips my hair into the thorns; ticks crawl along my arm.

I lean into the perfect order of everything growing wild, hold one more between my stained

fingers, walk across dusty gravel beneath humming power lines, drive home.

TO BARBARA KRUGER: MY BATTLEFIELD

Anna E. Childs

You say my face launched a thousand ships and here it is in Kruger's work, black and white
with rightful gray and darkness all around the eyes, and you always did want to rush

to blood for something—might as well be us. My boys say things like, "That's for girls,"
or "That's what girls do," nostrils flaring and eyes darting sideways,

as if toward a steel-colored sea just past the hill beside them. No matter how often I take hold
of the derision in their small voices, ten and six, trying to steer it back to see my eyes, my face,

I cannot make them want to *be* me, someone who bleeds monthly and lactates, soft,
rather than hard. Do I spank them into it, yell at them shrilly, return to the unyielding walls

put up again and again throughout the years, the eternal, halting hardness?
But isn't that what the ships were for—to sail across the edges into something more?

When I was thirty, before they were born, my body tricked me into believing there was life

inside it, my breasts and stomach swelling with summer sun and deeply greening leaves.

I rode each day swollen with the vision of myself at the height of what I was created to be,

softness stroked, honored, cherished like soft cloth tokens queens dropped to the ground.

Then life halted at some point, and inside became the black and white and gray
of an empty ultrasound picture with nothing truly there, with no reason for buoyancy,

for ships that sailed to the places I believed were there, beyond the edges of things.

And then the waking from the anesthesia under a blue sheet, believing I was dead,

because after all, there was my decision to end life, to allow a doctor's hands inside me,

inserting the vacuum, penetrating soft parts. And there were all the times at seventeen,

when I had sex and suspected life growing inside me, the plans to rise and launch
myself across state lines to find a clinic, to lie down, to take the hand of a nurse

like Sallie Tisdale, the plans I had to cry the tears, to say the goodbye, to take
a breath and rise up from the ground, hair swirling as I took a step, then another,

then crossed the whole world with my own bare feet. And since: the knowledge that the girl

always remains right there, eternally climbing from the table, walking into the world.

November 08, 2016: her face is on the sidewalk and there's a boot on her head.
September 18, 2020: the head of her is cut off, hair and glasses and eyes that read and see

and dissent—they roll away, down a hillside, to the sea. "I am a girl," I tell my sons,

"I stroked the plastic skin of my dolls, tucked them in beside me in my bed, brushed and brushed

their hair, tied pink ribbons, then pressed my feet into mud and grass, ran to climb a maple tree."

My sons laugh at me, tell me of course they love me, that I am different than the other girls,

yet they see in my eyes the rolling waves, gales moving in, shining rocks, mermaids. They

mount their bikes and leave, moving, clashing, clamoring through the darkness that remains.

SLOW

Madison Jozefiak

Today is a slow day.

Few customers. Heat waves, shimmering up from the pavement like a mirage. Even the smell of coffee, which I love to bury in my lungs, has gone rancid. The entire world is turning in slow motion, like a blue marble rotating in a jar of honey.

At seven o'clock, I ball up my apron and stuff it into my backpack. I say goodbye to Alexander. He grunts in reply. I leave through the front door of the coffeehouse, and the bell that sounds clear and silvery behind me is overtaken at once by the hissing of a manhole cover that issues a skinny jet of steam into the stuffy air. I've never done well in the heat, and this summer is threatening to eat me alive.

I live my days going back and forth between the coffeehouse and the apartment with its dysfunctional AC. My brain is boiling, and my sense of reality has long evaporated. I'm stuck with this constant floating sensation, a kind of freeing mental blankness that renders me unable to judge one thing from another—if someone tried to induct me into a cult right about now, they might succeed at it.

On my way home, I buy a milkshake from a fast-food joint. Three minutes later, it's reduced to a lukewarm sugar slurry. A fresh track list of lo-fi beats plays through my headphones as I walk along the set of abandoned tracks that snakes along the side of the main road. The rails are rusted and overgrown with green weeds. I've heard for the past five years that they're going to turn it into a bike path. The sun is on its way out, and the light it casts across the tracks is slanted, golden. This is the only thing I like about summer.

My shoelace comes untied, but I keep walking, marking my plastic straw with bite marks. My head is full of nothing but a spacey synth melody and a steady snare drum beat. There's a new text from my sister: *Going out tonight. Key at the bottom of the mailbox.*

Just then, my phone rings. I pull off my headphones, letting them hang around my neck.

"Hello?"

"Steven, this is Dana. What the hell is taking you so long?"

You have a voice that cuts, a clear and immediate sign of authority.

"Excuse me?" I say.

"The board meeting! You should've been here five minutes ago!"

"Oh. Sorry," I say, "I'll be there as soon as I can."

"You better fly like the wind," you growl, and hang up.

I pull my headphones back over my ears and continue to sip my milkshake through the straw.

My name is not Steven.

Every day the same. They pass as easily as pedestrians past the glass doors. The bell doesn't ring. I smile often, but I feel heavy. I feel like summer will never end. The pastries sink into themselves. The espresso machine is cleaned again and again with a wet rag for lack of any other work to do. The metal is so shiny it looks like it's sweating. My eyes flick to the headphones buried in my bag as I play music from memory.

Alexander asks about my life. My life is boring. Throughout the week, he tells me fragments of his vacation to Italy.

At seven o'clock, the heat is still unbearable, and I'm wearing jeans. Long pants required to work at the coffeehouse. Close-toed shoes, and a plain black apron. I haven't seen my older sister in a few days. When a heatwave comes, she rides on the back of it. She goes far away. The key is always hidden in a new place.

Under the stack of old magazines. Beneath the third rock to the left of the steps. Stuck between the flowerpots on the neighbor's front porch.

Sometimes I wonder if I really have an older sister, or if I just imagined her.

I get a call from you every now and then, and you're never happy with me. You condemn my lateness and demand all sorts of things: documents, reports, doughnuts. You tell me I am *irresponsible* for not participating in the group survey, *inadequate* for contributing so little to the latest project. The words wedge themselves into the cracks of my self-esteem. I think if I were really Steven, I'd be cripppled.

One day, you call as I'm waiting for the bus. The heat is worse than ever, and I'm going out of my mind with the repetition of the days. Still, I take off my headphones for you as always.

"I won't continue to tolerate this kind of behavior in my office," you say. "Maybe you don't realize your position. I have just as much authority as Joe, now, and if you can't reconcile with that—"

"Look," I cut in, "you don't know me, and you really don't know what I'm going through."

"*Excuse me*?" Your tone could make a stone flinch. "What I know is that you should've been at the meeting this morning with everyone else!"

I exhale.

"Sorry. I was out of line."

"Clearly."

"It's been a tough couple of weeks. You have to understand."

"...That's alright."

There's the sound of shuffling. Maybe you're switching the phone to your other ear.

"I can't remember the last time we spoke in person. How about you come to my office after tomorrow's meeting? We can talk one-on-one."

"That's the thing. Like I said...You don't *know* me." Sadness creeps into my voice. "I'm not Steven."

"What?"

As the bus pulls up, I'm filled with horror. This could be our last conversation, and the end of the only thing that happened to me this summer.

"Sorry, Dana," I say. I hang up on you for the first time.

I pull my headphones back on. There's a new song, just as mellow as the one before. Lo-fi is almost an antidote for this heat, but not quite.

Key underneath the trashcan out back, says my sister's text.

Leftover radiation oozes off my skin as I lie in bed that night. I can picture you easily every time I close my eyes. In your realm of glossy skyscrapers, you are manager or CEO on the 50th floor. Everything is neatly compartmentalized into working and eating and meeting spaces. Even the light that filters in through the glass must be cleaner than what's outside. And you're the director, the puppet master. You live in a world I can only imagine. Not better, I think, than my own; and not any worse, just different. I would give anything to have just one day that's different.

I fall asleep with my headphones on.

A week later, as I'm taking the bus to work, I watch the clouds. They're huge floating islands, substantial enough to leave shadows. My thoughts feel several stories above my head. The financial district is a few blocks away from the coffeehouse, and I'm convinced you work in the building with sunflowers in the side garden.

Emily points to a spot of sweetened condensed milk on the counter, a tiny white disc. I grab a dish rag. Few customers. Business is slow as usual. Emily starts chatting about the shocking outcome of the latest World Cup match. I didn't know she liked soccer, but I like your voice better, so when I get a call from you, I always answer.

"Hello?"

"I'm sitting at my desk," you say.

"OK," I say.

I picture you, sitting at your desk.

"I have the company address book in front of me."

Adding that to my mental image. I wonder where this is going.

"Which department are you from?"

"Department?"

"Are you from Marketing? I always confused the people from Marketing."

In a slow-burning world where all the edges are melted down, your voice is sharp as crystal.

"What did you say your name was?"

"I didn't say. It's Matthew."

"Matthew..."

I glance towards the glass doors as I hear you flip the page.

"Sorry for confusing you with Steven. I have the right number for him, now."

You pause.

"Is everything alright?"

"Hmm?"

"I sensed that something was troubling you, last we spoke."

"It's nothing really," I say at once.

You're quiet on the other end, waiting. I hold my breath, half-expecting the bell on the door to ring and break me off.

"It's just my sister," I say, finally. "She's gone missing."

I haven't seen Anïse in weeks. The texts stopped coming three days ago. Now the key stays wherever I leave it.

"Oh," you say softly. "That's horrible."

"It's not like that," I say, now regretting my choice of words.

"You must be terrified."

"It could mean nothing. It could mean she's only enjoying herself more than usual."

My sister might be halfway around the world by now. Taken any train, hitchhiked, even stolen a car. She has found her way, before, to a month-long string of parties and raves she wasn't invited to. I won't complain as long as she sends money home.

"The last time I saw her was at the end of July," I say. "Her face was floating above me when I woke up, wrapped in this red scarf that glowed like lava. I think she said, 'There's a heat wave coming. Are you going to be okay?' But I was still half asleep; one step out of a dream where I rode an overheated train through the desert, on and on. I thought I might be imagining her. I saw she had two packed bags, one under each arm, and when I woke up again, she wasn't there anymore.

What's so funny?"

"Nothing," you say, muffling laughter.

"My sister spirals into recklessness in the summer, Dana. Neither of us are good with the heat; but me, I slow down. Everything slows down."

"You have a way with words," you say. "You *are* from Marketing, right?"

"I'm not," I say.

"No?"

"I don't work at your company."

You fall silent on the other end of the line. After all the harsh words I've endured on Steven's behalf, this silence is the thing that might break me.

Moments later, I'm staring blankly ahead and resting my knuckles against the counter. A customer comes in, the first one all day. He asks for iced coffee. I tell him I was just about to make some. I only have to brew it fresh and cool it down in the fridge. How long will that take, he wants to know. Only a couple of hours.

After he leaves, I go digging through my backpack for my headphones. You might have said something before I hung up, but I wasn't listening. There's a writhing in my chest, a feeling I hate. Emily comes back from the bathroom and unwraps a stick of blue gum. And the day continues.

In the three days that follow, a historic heatwave strikes the city.

Fires break out, ponds evaporate, and public waterworks are dry as bone. Incidents of heatstroke skyrocket. There's an eerie orange tinge to the horizon. People cook sunny-side-up eggs on the pavement and post the videos online. We all know what this means—liquidated ice caps, rising sea levels, mass extinction, all things that could have been avoided were it not for human nature hastening the end of the world. As for me, I can't remember anything from the time of the heat wave. The rubber soles of my sneakers have melted from the rails of the train tracks, so I must have walked to work. Those three days are nothing but a white flash, leaving me with only a vague recollection of smoke rising up in several turrets from the city and the high-pitched wail of fire engines.

When I come to, everything is different. The heat has ebbed. I'm walking home from work, and the train tracks don't look the same without the golden light of a cloudless evening.

Is summer finally ending?

There's a threatening rumble from the clouds. I pull on my headphones, and a few minutes later, it's pouring. My socks are drenched, every step squeezes out liquid that is instantly replaced. I reach my building and walk up the steps at an even pace. Once I'm inside, I leave the lights off and throw my bag and headphones on the carpet. I strip away the wet pieces of clothing, one by one, like unwrapping a mummy shell. Then I open the widow. I take a deep breath; raking wet hair out of my eyes. Like waking up from a dream, the heat has come to an end.

Once my phone dries out, I see that I have one missed call and a new voicemail message. Both are from you.

"Matthew, this is Dana. I just heard your voicemail."

Voicemail? When did I leave a voicemail?

"I'm... not sure what to say. I didn't realize you saw me that way. Make no mistake—I don't appreciate being lied to. But I'm deeply concerned for you, whoever you are. Call me again."

My palms are suddenly damp with perspiration. I have no memory at all during the heatwave. I could very well have called and left you a message. Christ, what did I say? I regain control of my breathing, and then I replay your voicemail, to remember the way it sounds.

Call me again.

I tuck the sound of your voice into a pocket of my memory, then delete it from my phone. The heat is over. That means I can manage without you.

The day's downpour turns into a persistent drizzle that lasts the rest of the week. I go to and from the coffeehouse, and I don't mind it as much as before. I bring an umbrella, and I look forward to my walks in the fresh air.

At the end of the week, I get a call from my sister as I'm watching TV.

"I thought you were dead," I say.

"Please, Matty," she replies. "I'm invincible, like God or a cockroach."

On the screen, a lawyer lifts a red-stained evidence baggie, and the jury recoils.

"Are you at home?" Anïse says. "I need you to check something for me."

"I haven't heard from you in weeks," I say.

"Were you worried?"

"No."

"Good. Love you, too. Now, go check my room."

Once I confirm that the white leather skirt she describes is underneath her bed, she lets out a string of curses.

"OK," she says when she's finished. "See you next week." She hangs up.

See you next week?

Where the hell is she?

The last week of August arrives along with the procession of rain clouds. On the first of September, there's a small going away party for me and Emily. We're both attending college nearby and have campus jobs during the school year.

Emily is gluten free, and so is the cake. The taste is almost identical to cardboard. But it doesn't matter. The weather is perfect, cool and fresh, and Alexander wishes us the best of luck. We sit at a small round table in front of the shop. The sky is bright and clouds pass over at a frantic pace, hopelessly caught in a celestial current. I point this out to my coworkers, and we stare for a while.

Just then, a sleek black car pulls up in front of us, sliding along the curb. I notice its windows are tinted. It stops a little way down the street in a 30-minute parking spot. A tall woman, even taller in heels, steps out. She walks towards us.

"Are you open?"

"Sorry. We're closed for lunch. Fifteen more minutes."

I don't look up from the blue frosting on my paper plate, but my shoulders stiffen. She sighs.

"Fifteen minutes? I've never been late, before. I guess there's a first time for everything."

Knowing what I have to do, every half-second I keep my eyes fixed on the plate is a procrastination. I lift my head to look at her.

You're in your early forties, narrow face, high cheekbones, eyes bright with that exact element I always heard in your voice: cool clarity. Everything about your appearance is impeccable. A straight black skirt, a crisp white collar. Golden hoop earrings. The way your long hair is styled. Clean nails, manicured, beige. You're self-designed down to the last detail. You're beautiful, of course.

"Hello, Matthew."

At first I'm shocked as to how you've recognized me, until I realize it must be the look on my face. Mortified, I force a smile.

"Hi."

"Is this where you work, Matthew?"

"That's right."

"And you like it here?"

"Sure."

"They treat you well here?"

"Absolutely."

"Hmm."

You nod, apparently satisfied. Everyone else at the table is speechless. They look from you to me. And back again.

"Everyone, this is Dana," I say. "She's my… um… Well, she's…" I rise to my feet. "Dana, do you want anything to drink?"

Alexander looks at me.

"Matt..."

"It's fine," I say. "She'll be late for her meeting, otherwise." I turn back to you. "What would you like?"

You tap a long-nailed finger to your jawline.

"Large soy iced latte, half decaf. With cinnamon, if you have it."

"Sounds good," I say.

We head inside. I grab a clear plastic cup from behind the counter.

"Sorry for interrupting your party," you say.

"That's OK."

"What's it for?"

"Me. And my coworker—it's a going-away party, for the end of summer."

"Hmm."

"How did you find me?" I ask.

You lean your elbows against the counter.

"Is it the end of summer, already? My vacation time keeps piling up."

I finish brewing the decaf shot and dump it into the cup.

"I'm amazed, actually," you say, "You're just a kid."

This is a comment that leaves me feeling slightly singed on the inside, but I try not to show it as I scoop the ice. I keep my hands busy; I don't look at you.

"You seemed much older, on the phone."

I don't know what to say. You look like I expected. Or at the very least, now that I've seen you, I can't imagine you looking any other way. I'm unwilling to meet your eyes, but you swivel to find mine anyway when I pass you the iced latte.

"Do you really like working here?"

"It's fine," I say.

"Just fine?"

"It's the same thing every day. Other than that, though. No complaints."

"Why didn't you call me back?"

I swallow dryly, but when I look at you, there's nothing unsteady about it.

"I didn't have any reason to."

"Really?"

"You don't need to worry about me."

"What about your sister?"

"She called. She's fine."

You pause, and I detect both warmth and exasperation in your silence.

"Maybe there isn't a reason." When you lean forward, your smile is entirely at odds with your air of authority. "Who cares? I want to take you somewhere."

There's that writhing feeling again, like my heart is twisting to fill a new space that's given way unexpectedly in my chest.

"What do you mean? Take me where?"

"I don't know. Somewhere different."

"Right now?"

"Sure."

"What about your meeting?"

"They'll survive without me."

I think I see the light shift to its slanted, golden form. I think the light changes when I'm around you.

"Where do you want to go?" you say, the first of many times. "I'll give you a ride."

The air is clean and the clouds are moving quickly. My headphones are sitting in the same spot where I left them on the carpet. The rainwater has evaporated, and they haven't moved.

It feels like summer is over.

I couldn't be more relieved.

THE TERRORISTS

Marisa P. Clark

That September Tuesday, my parents called
 en route to New Mexico from Mississippi, by way
of the Dakotas. Mom's first words: *We lost a lot*

of money today. They'd been turned away
 at Mount Rushmore, but not to worry: *We saw it*
from the outside. My father took the phone:

We need to bomb the hell out of them, and do it now,
 before those bleeding-heart Democrat liberals waste
time trying to talk things out. True, civilians will die—

but that's to be expected. We need to bomb them
 flat. An Air Force veteran, he'd seen combat,
but only on TV. All day I'd listened to the president

preach of good and evil, as if to paraphrase a Bible
 dumbed down just for him, his lips aquiver
with a wish to lift into a smile every time he mentioned

war. He threatened strikes against those who harbored
 terrorists. Come Thursday, my parents arrived
in a Chrysler minivan. *It's Patriotic Blue, the blue*

of the flag, my mother raved when they'd bought it.
          I expected to see the flag sag half-mast
from the antenna, like every other jingoistic cliché

driving our country's highways, but instead,
          they'd bought a license plate of a bald eagle's head
superimposed across the stars and stripes. The guts

of insects spattered it, a massacre of travel.
          I harbored my parents for days. It sickened them
to see me cry. They feared I'd lose my job

if I dared disagree aloud with the good
          ol' boys in charge. We couldn't talk without
fighting, so we watched TV. We watched reruns

of low-flying planes, fireballs, and tall buildings
          falling until, mercifully, the cable went out. They
stayed long enough for it to come back on, to show

Wall Street ring its opening bell. They watched stocks
          plummet fast and hard. Then we said goodbye. They
cried. Backed out and turned those two emblems

of the USA toward the future and its promise
          of mass casualties. Collateral damage.

CONTRIBUTORS

James Tadd Adcox's work has appeared in *Granta, n+1,* and *Passages North,* among other places. He's the author of a novel, *Does Not Love,* and a novella, *Repetition,* and is a founding editor at the literary magazine *Always Crashing.*

Gabriel Blackwell is the author of five books, the most recent of which is *Babel* (Splice, 2020). His next book, *CORRECTION,* will be out in spring 2021 from Rescue Press. He is the editor of *The Rupture.*

Ryan Bollenbach is a writer and musician living in Houston, Texas. He formerly served as poetry editor for *Black Warrior Review* in Tuscaloosa, Alabama. He reads for *Gulf Coast* and *Heavy Feather Review.* His writing has appeared or is forthcoming in *Tarpaulin Sky Magazine, Sink Review, Painted Bride Quarterly, Snail Trail Press,* and elsewhere. Reach out on twitter @SilentAsIAm.

K. Branagan is a writer and artist from the Ohio Valley. She received a Bachelor of Science from Kent State University in 2016 and currently resides in Steubenville, Ohio, where she works as a library assistant.

Michael Buckius is a writer and filmmaker from Lancaster, PA. His work has appeared in *Ghost City Review, Masque and Spectacle, Shrew, Write On, Downtown,* and elsewhere. His first chapbook, *Future Sarcasm,* is available now from Tolsun Books.

Juliana Chang is a Taiwanese-American poet. She is the 2019 recipient of the Urmy/Hardy Poetry Prize, the 2017 recipient of the Wiley Birkhofer Poetry Prize, and a 2015 Scholastic Gold Medalist in Poetry. Her work appears in *The Chestnut Review, Okay Donkey, The Scores, The Best Teen Writing of 2015,* and elsewhere. Her debut chapbook, *Inheritance,* is forthcoming with Paper Nautilus Press in 2021.

Anna E. Childs is a poet and college English instructor from East Tennessee. Her love for poetry began when her father, also a professor, gave her his *Norton Anthologies* and she began copying by hand all of the poems that struck a chord with her. This led to eventually filling notebooks with her own verse. Her poetry most recently appeared in *The Adirondack Review* and *2River View.*

Marisa P. Clark is a queer Southerner whose writing appears in *Shenandoah, Cream City Review, Nimrod, Epiphany, Foglifter, Potomac Review, Rust + Moth, Louisiana Literature,* and elsewhere. *Best American Essays 2011* recognized her nonfiction among its Notable Essays. She lives in New Mexico with three parrots and two dogs.

Arthur Davis has had over a hundred original tales published in eighty journals. He was featured in a single author anthology, nominated for a Pushcart Prize, received the 2018 Write Well Award for excellence in short fiction and, twice nominated, received Honorable Mention in *The Best American Mystery Stories 2017.*

Hollie Dugas lives in Louisiana. Her work has been selected to be included in *Barrow Street, Reed Magazine, Crab Creek Review, Redivider, Pembroke, Salamander, Poet Lore, Watershed Review, Whiskey Island, Chiron Review, Louisiana Literature,* and *CALYX.* Most recently, Hollie has been nominated for the 2020 Pushcart Prize.

Joachim Glage lives and writes in Colorado, where he also enjoys no longer being an attorney. Some of Glage's other writings, which seek to explore the boundaries of fiction itself, have appeared recently, or are forthcoming, in issues of *The Georgia Review, Litmag, Santa Monica Review, Juked, The Rupture, The Moth, Heavy Feather Review,* and other periodicals.

Madison Jozefiak studied English and creative writing at Colgate University in Upstate New York. She lives outside of Boston where she now spends her time reading Kafka, amassing knowledge of the healthcare system, and biking through the cold along the Charles River. She is oddly addicted to the innocuous jazz music heard in cafés.

Michael Martone's new book is *The Complete Writings of Art Smith, the Bird Boy of Fort Wayne, Edited by Michael Martone* published by BOA Editions LTD. He lives in Tuscaloosa and has retired from teaching after 40 years.

Evan McHenry is a high school senior at Bishop Seabury Academy in Lawrence, KS. He writes for the school newspaper and plays varsity soccer. In his free time, Evan can be found shooting astrophotography at night and catching up on sleep during the day.

Sonnet Mondal is an Indian poet, photographer, and author of *Karmic Chanting* (Copper Coin 2018) and *Ink and Line* (Dhauli Books 2018). Founder/director of Chair Poetry Evenings - Kolkata's International Festival, Mondal edits the Indian section of *Lyrikline* (House of Poetry, Berlin). His works have been translated into over fifteen languages.

Elizabeth Moore graduated from Washburn in 2020 and now works for the National Association of Trailer Manufacturers as an editor. This is her first publication.

Brianna Noll is the author of *The Era of Discontent*, forthcoming from Elixir Press in 2021, and *The Price of Scarlet*, named one of the top poetry books of 2017 by the *Chicago Review of Books*. Poetry editor of *The Account*, she lives in Los Angeles.

Brian Oliu teaches, writes, and fights out of Tuscaloosa, Alabama. His publications include three chapbooks and five full-length collections of nonfiction, ranging on topics from Craigslist Missed Connections, to computer viruses, to the *Rocky* film series, to the arcade game *NBA Jam*. His newest book of essays, *Body Drop: Notes on Fandom and Pain in Professional Wrestling*, is forthcoming in 2021 by The University of North Carolina Press.

James Rogers lives in New York and is a teacher at the United Nations International School. Originally from Ireland, his short fiction has appeared in *The First Line, The Galway Review* and *Close to the Bone.*

Gregor Southard is a native of Topeka, Kansas. After graduating from the University of Kansas with a degree in Theatre and Film Production, he moved to Nashville to pursue a career as a writer and a filmmaker. He has had several short stories and poems published over the years and wrote or co-wrote plays that were produced in Nashville and a musical in Denver.

Bradley R. Strahan taught poetry at Georgetown University. He has six books of poetry & over 700 poems published worldwide. His two latest books, *This Art of Losing* and *A Parting Glass* (his book of poems written in Ireland) were both translated into French.

Jeremy Szuder; 15 years as a musician, graphic design work, 25 years of self published Zines, fine art, 10 years deejaying, and continues to have illustrations and poems published by fine art and literary publications across the U.S.A. and Canada. He lives in Glendale, California.

Brooke Wonders is an Associate Professor at the University of Northern Iowa. Her work has appeared in *Clarkesworld, The Rupture,* and *Black Warrior Review,* among others. She serves as nonfiction editor at the *North American Review* and is a founding editor of *Grimoire Magazine.*

Lierin Woods is a Washburn University graduate with a B.A. in English. Her poetry has been published in *The Merrimack Review* and she was awarded the 2019 Judith Jacobson Traxler Award for Excellence in Writing.